WATER QUALITY

THE HUGH MACLENNAN POETRY SERIES

Editors: Allan Hepburn and Carolyn Smart

Recent titles in the series

Water Quality

CYNTHIA WOODMAN KERKHAM

McGill-Queen's University Press

Montreal & Kingston • London • Chicago

ISBN 978-0-2280-2297-8 (paper)
ISBN 978-0-2280-2344-9 (ePDF)
ISBN 978-0-2280-2345-6 (ePUB)

Legal deposit fourth quarter 2024
Bibliothèque nationale du Québec

Printed in Canada on acid-free paper that is 100% ancient forest free
(100% post-consumer recycled), processed chlorine free

Funded by the Government of Canada   Financé par le gouvernement du Canada | Canadä   Canada Council for the Arts   Conseil des arts du Canada

We acknowledge the support of the Canada Council for the Arts.

Nous remercions le Conseil des arts du Canada de son soutien.

McGill-Queen's University Press in Montreal is on land which long served
as a site of meeting and exchange amongst Indigenous Peoples, including
the Haudenosaunee and Anishinabeg nations. In Kingston it is situated
on the territory of the Haudenosaunee and Anishinaabek. We acknowledge
and thank the diverse Indigenous Peoples whose footsteps have marked
these territories on which peoples of the world now gather.

Library and Archives Canada Cataloguing in Publication

Title: Water quality / Cynthia Woodman Kerkham.

Names: Woodman Kerkham, Cynthia, author.

Series: Hugh MacLennan poetry series.

Description: Series statement: The Hugh MacLennan poetry series

Identifiers: Canadiana (print) 20240396278 | Canadiana (ebook)
20240396286 | ISBN 9780228022978 (softcover) |
ISBN 9780228023449 (PDF) | ISBN 9780228023456 (ePUB)

Subjects: LCGFT: Poetry.

Classification: LCC PS8645.O6384 W38 2024 | DDC C811/.6—dc23

This book was typeset by Marquis Interscript in 9.5/13 Sabon.
Copyediting by Alyssa Favreau.

For Grayson and Hunter,
love ubiquitous

All the flowers are forms of water.
~ W.S. Merwin, "Rain Light"

CONTENTS

Contents

Contents

FORK LAKE

*For the Friends of Fork Lake, who share a front
yard with kindness and grace*

Wildness challenges us with the irony that self-willed places
will only continue through our will.

~ Roger Kaye, Arctic National Wildlife Refuge

WATER QUALITY

She bends to the service of water,
lowers a Secchi disk until its white disappears,
notes the depth. Again and again reading turbidity.

    April and she wears a short wetsuit. Belly and
      chest warmed,
    she ducks her head – thrill of cold zippers her spine.

Feeder creek and spring-fed, this lake. Gouged by glaciers.
Eighteen homes now people its patient shore,
it's shared front yard, no space for more.

    Water gloves her body in late June.
    Satin, yes, viscous. Albumen, vernix, newborn slick.

Tests wash light on columns of lake, measure algae-haze, weed.
Secchi disk dipped below the surface
spins from glass to grey to gone. Speechless water speaking.

    Sweet water, not leaf, not stone, but
    soft, rain soft. Something to husband.

The samples say this water's pretty good: phosphates,
nitrates at acceptable levels. Coliforms and aquatic flora
(pondweed and long-stemmed water-shield): a titch up.

    July dusk and spent midges fleck the top inch.
    Breaststroke is parting curtains of small beads.

Suckled on lead of city taps,
some friends won't swim. They balk at bugs,
at trout, and bottom mud.

Fly corpses sink, swallowed by cutthroats.
Dive deep to spring source, sluice.

Some prefer a pool in blue tile
where chlorine nibbles
layers of protein from the skin.

Late August night, naked, full-mooned, her body swims
inside a blood-warm caress. Mammalian hug. Rolling
in mink.

This place she's lived fifty years.
She is water strider.
Light prints. A whisper of strokes.

Fall and the shy garter pops its periscopic head,
rare glide along a velvet floss of lake.

Canoes congregate
where *Nymphaea odorata*
spills from Mount Work Park,
chokes swimming, clogs drinking water,
and shrinks the lake. So we garden –
from a boat, drop a cutter deep to the roots,
then land-footed neighbours pull and drag
along the bottom, leaving mats
of thin red stalks, broken veins,
for paddlers to rake and haul
into their boats till gunwales
barely skim the water line,
and we dump the piles on shore.
My peach-painted toes squelch in mud,
I lug huge green and purple leaves,
my hands slimed by gelatinous undersides:
something translucent, beetle-shaped clings
beside a cluster of eggs – freshwater shrimp?
Rosy red minnow? I fling the creature back
to the lake. Leave its jellied babies,
their centres dark in gluey sacs,
to die in the sun.

We sit in a circle of twenty-five, neighbours whose homes
ring this lake, asking what to do about the old cedars
dying of thirst. Now unable to shield the lake from the
siphoning sun, the cedars wave rusty scarves of despair.
We've called in an expert on weirs: low dams to regulate
water flow, to keep the lake level up, keep roots wet in
summer, prevent flooding in winter. The circle shivers
in mid-June cold. Some say our actions put us in this
mess so best to withdraw. Others mount arguments in full
barding – sheathed in the shine of statistics – this battle of
our making, they say, only our making can undo; nothing
natural anymore in this post-wilderness. Lake as shared
front yard now shrinking and the gardeners want to
install a small weir. The guardians want to do nothing.
Talk floats up and up as stars call down in ancestral
whispers. Those who want to ride to battle, those who
want to watch. We all agree, death dries the air. But is it
destruction or simply change? *Shut up*, the man beside
me hurls at the visiting expert on weirs – they're old
friends, but still. The cold freezing blood now, freezing
fingers and the meeting ends. We pile chairs, chat round
a table. One neighbour's chocolate cookies, another's
Bing cherries in the growing dark.

lake-cool breeze drops
sprays of brittle cedar leaves
small gusts of laughter

RECIPE FOR INVASIVE SPECIES

The best way to eat a bullfrog,
American, that is, is to soak

those plump thighs in soya sauce and ginger, or
red wine with garlic and sear on the barbeque.

Released into the lake system
by some chef who had these ideas.

First you must hunt and freeze
their twenty-thousand-egg-sliming-

baby-duck-and-lime-green-
endangered-tree-frog-gobbling bodies.

Headlamps and spears are required.
You track them by their ailing-bovine croak.

Spearman in the bow,
paddler in the stern.

Slow glide into reeds.
Gash of paralyzing light.

The skewered bullfrog
bagged in clove oil to anesthetise

then plopped into a freezer
for that slow drift into forever sleep.

You can, by the way, add lime to the marinade
or a dash of lemon, a splash of vinegar.

Though the full-grown frog
is the size of a large dinner plate,

the thighs are slim. Turn frequently.
They cook fast on the grill.

Keep basting, and be prepared
for all to remark how much they taste like chicken.

Beaver chew the lake's alder, and blue-green algae scums
   the shore.
The lake drops more each summer. Floods higher some
   winters.
Parched trees, drowned docks. Always this battle.

Locals talk about old Gregory, first settler,
digging a trench, lowering the water level
for his sheep. Such hubris, we now think.

Steward, from old English: ward of the house, the hall.
Always changing the locks, calling for repairs,
we jangle the keys to the larder.

Should we construct a weir on the trench?
Control lake levels the way old Gregory did –
or leave well enough alone?

The Friends of Fork Lake have bought the beavers
a special pipe so they can build, but not block,
willing to sacrifice some alder to the national rodent. Not all.

Evening sun blankets the docks, and in the hush
flutter and click of ducks stripping aphids from aquatic grass.
A mink wrinkles the lake surface gold, torpedoes a webbed foot –

     animals and their fine-tuned destruction.

This morning on the dock, a tiny spider weaves
between slats of a cedar chair.
I'm trapped by ordinary fear.

> Years ago someone dumped a car,
> a hunk of rusted metal, gas, and oil
> in the middle of this lake.

Aranea diadema. Were she human-sized, her cartwheel web
would need four hundred yards of silk.
To grasp such magnitude.

> July sun unsticks itself from treetops.
> Dragonflies zip lines of blue and black.
> Fish hawk plunges, dazzles.

Six spinnerets – teats with six hundred taps –
pour five different silks, and then add glue
from two more special spouts.

> Praise learning about spiders
> and other fearful things, praise
> the calm it brings.

She holds a string of silk aloft with one hind leg,
exudes oil to unstick her foot,
then plucks on the glue-limed line.

The car never pulled from the lake
has rotted away. The guns
that once shot hawks, silenced.

The spider ties, glues, twangs the gummed line
so each drop of glue separates
into equidistant beads.

O to be more careful:
web torn from its moorings
as I drag the chair.

But the spider comes scurrying, shoots
a repairing thread from her upthrust belly
to take hold where the wind will land it.

Mayflies jig above the lake surface, dizzy with their one-day life. Late sun squints a slow warmth. I sit in silence on the dock and listen – clank of wind chimes: antique forks and spoons outside a kitchen window down the lake.

mountain road
smoke curls
into hushed blue

A man tried to find silence once, went to mountain cave dwellings, then underground, and, in a lead-lined room, was disturbed to hear his heartbeat. John Cage makes music from stillness. I don't seek the anechoic – just wind clacking spears of yellow water iris, clatter of dragonfly wing in brief collision with its neighbour, the night music of treefrogs. Who am I but a second-homer with a family history here since '52? I won't ask the lady down the lake to dismantle her waving cutlery. Won't complain to the neighbour who hosts rock-band practice Tuesday nights. I'll slip on orange plastic earmuffs, as if on a construction site. Wait for the heavy metal to subside.

winter storm
in a quiet library
blinds rattle

The guy next door says: *there are those who want quiet, and those who think now they're outside the city, they can do whatever the hell they want.* His predecessor by decades blasted the granite boulder at the lip of the lake, kept the cement mixer going for a year, then mounted a tiny lighthouse to snick at blinking intervals – me; me; me. On a summer moonlit night, someone swam naked to the point, yanked the lighthouse off its pedestal, carted it to town.

calm evening
from a porch across the lake
clink of knife on plate

On our acre of unplugged, I crack ears with axe chops, scrape a bucket against the dock. Dip then haul, and, on occasion, bring out a chain saw. Join the snarling chorus.

sudden March sun
the backlit drip
of snow

The lake named for the fork,
the way water branched west,
cradled marsh, mallard, mink.

Farmer Gregory, the first settler
sliding his skiff along lake bends
pulling on parallel oars

as mist lifted from fern, rush, sedge.
And at night, skimming his palm
along his wife's hip.

Gregory claiming the lake so fully
he felt he could undo it –
could blast and dig for two years

a wide trench to siphon water downstream,
drop the lake level by ten feet,
creating pasture for his sheep.

Call it dereliction: *a recession*
of water leaving dry land.
Call it settler spirit. Call it

Fork Lake, unforked.
And at night with his wife,
rivulet of seed.

SPILL

Smoke from distant forest fires gauzes a red sun, tints
the morning lake. Before Bic lighters, before friction
matches, Londoners kept a fire going somewhere in the
house, kept twists of paper, or thin strips of wood as spills
to start from an old fire a new one to banish the chill.
In the kitchen, say, or the bedroom. A vase on the
mantelpiece full of spills. Fast forward to the nineteen-
fifties, into colonial histories, Ken, a logger by trade,
clears a slash pile in a field of fallen trees in the Highland
district of Vancouver Island using as his spill an orange
crush bottle with a rag stopper. Amber bottle full of
gasoline. The Great Fire of London started on a Sunday
in a baker's shop on Pudding Lane. Wind spilling fire
down Fish Lane down to the shores of the Thames,
buildings burning until Wednesday. And wind spills Ken's
slash fire, too, into trees, onto farms, down to the edge
of Fork Lake where the deer take refuge. The peat bog
under Bolton's farm smoulders afterwards for two
hollowing years. Sir Christopher Wren planned new
churches, new bakeries, sprouting a new city over thirty
years. In the woods, ephemerals come first – wildflowers,
fireweed – then grasses, quick trees – aspen and birch.
Decades on, tall conifers. Christmas trees for sale now
on Bolton's farm. And this morning, wildfires flood the
province. Singed orange light stumbles across the lake.
Smoke burns throats, veils again the high red eye.

After a cave-deep sleep in the family cabin,
I stand on the dock. Sunbeams splinter
the rippling lake, and I think of lives
taken for country, for duty, pleasure, pay –
shot   poisoned   drowned.
Sun shatters crystals across the dark sweep of lake,
now burning my face, now gone   as wind shifts
and the planet turns in her wandering.
It's Remembrance Day, but no silence
from the man next door, drilling through granite.
I think he might stop at the eleventh hour
of the eleventh day of the eleventh month, but he doesn't.
He keeps right on drilling high up the hill for water,
keeps boring a hole
through the earth's friable chest.

LIVE TRAP

In the mornings, I take the trap
to the edge of the park, flip the tin lid –
brown mouse, barely the size
of a pinecone, black glass eyes.
Virtuous as a conscientious objector,
I use a live spider trap, too – sliding
Plexiglas panels for easy entrapment
and, with a twist of the wrist, easy release.
Same tool for wasps. A friend suggested
I plant it beside the bowl of potato salad.
Even one wasp inside flails with enough distress
it warns others off. I watch it struggle
against its clear prison, buzz and bash itself
to exhaustion – question my kindness.
Today I smushed a wolf spider in the sink
with a ball of paper towel. Was I surprised?
Angry at something? It was automatic –
grab, rip, crush – brown smear
on white porcelain, swiped then tossed in the trash.
And tonight, mouse, if you rattle me awake again,
will I take you to the lake and drop you in?

BORDER CONTROL

~ for Lin

Fizzle Lake reports they've cleaned out all breeding adult
Bullfrogs and juveniles this year after hunting for three
weeks straight   all olive-green-blotched-with-brownish
markings-white-bellied-spotted-with-yellow or gray
gone   similar news for Fork Lake all breeding adults
certainly calling males   silenced   at worst there
might be an escaped juvenile at Fizzle   and a
subversive Red-legged frog *was* seen sitting very near a
Bullfrog for a few nights in a row   will we see Red-
legged bullfrogs in the future?   Identifying the enemy
isn't as easy as you might think. In the dark, in a canoe,
the spear chucker poised at the bow   search lamp
sheening the undersides of alder leaves   the glossy
plates of lily pads   spotlight reflecting from eyeballs
at lake level their eye shine like two fat pearls afloat
or is that an adult Red-legs?   Search for the larger
tympanic membrane   colour difference   Fizzle
Lake also has the Green frog   mid-sized   not to be
confused with the Pacific tree frog which is also green but
lime and smaller   the Green frog definitely not to be
confused with the similarly mottled juvenile Bullfrog
while it's true the Green frog is not native and was
imported from the East it seems to croak in concert with
the locals so for now deemed native not invasive   not
to be confused with   not on the list

SECOND LAKE REPORT

Wildflowers in spring (shooting star, fawn lily,
    satin-flower)
considered native because we've no record

of when or how they arrived by bird drop or human foot.
This property, mostly undisturbed,

purchased by the Land Conservancy.
Now the Friends of Second Lake

rid the lacustrine, the forest and bluff
of Eastern water lilies, the pink ones,

(the larger-leafed, considered native,
a single fist of yellow bloom).

Eradicate gorse, Laurel-leaved Daphne,
English holly, English hawthorn, Scotch broom.

Dig out Canada thistle, thought, in fact,
to be originally from the Mediterranean.

No dogs permitted at present. And few people.
The Friends leave archeological features intact:

fencing (except loose barbed wire) from settler homes,
settler barns. No record of earlier human disturbance.

A rotted car, dumped in the middle of the lake in the
fifties, floats to the surface – rusty yellow, dented, now
dripping and gleaming, gutted of oil. A girl and her
grandmother swim out to it, stroke the weeds skirting
its frame. They open the doors and clamber in, marvel in
the half-submerged seats – the girl at the steering wheel,
her hand on the gearshift. Across the flat lake, a young
father talks to his son from their quiet porch. *Don't kill
spiders*, he says, *they're necessary*. The gentle boy carries
the spider outside; the girl, sequined in droplets, beams
from the driver's seat.

I SIP A GLASS OF WINE BY THE LAKE

~ for JK and QK, always

To contemplate the busy life: fish flip,
dragonfly float. Ducks on a log jutting
from shore, gilded by the sun's evening dip,
preening copper breasts, the breeze soft falling.

Evergreens double on lake's perfect glass.
Trout rise to mayflies, remembrance follows:
our children, their upturned, bobbing faces
haloed by sun, orange lifejacket collars,

their scramble onto inflatable rafts
game of sharks, push off then rescue with brave
screams of delight from imagined traps –
those preservers with loops I'd pull to save.

How they swim for me now in this lake's hold,
lost time-as-one held in mind's rippled folds.

LAKE GHAZAL

In the early evening cascade of warm light,
little bouncing flies ambered in golden light.

I'm old as cedar's leafless lower branches
shorn by the shade of young limbs eating light.

Sun presses cheek, then lips – a lover!
All I need now is this caress of light.

A buzz by my ear so quick I miss it's shape –
primal insect fear: a place without light.

Ripples like tiny sunboats rocking,
water's stroke on the rowboat hull sounds light.

Caddisfly cuddles in mud before flight.
When sperm ignites egg, zinc flash of first light.

Liquid canvas, a flat sun/moon reflected.
How water sheds itself in fluid light

at the lake. I believe a god is here.
When Cynthia asks, the answer is light.

WEDDING

August evening getting ready
for a summer shindig
and the lake never disappoints,
sparkles under a hot blue canopy.

> Lake spring-fed by snowmelt
> from Olympic Mountains, tunnelling
> under sea-weight of Juan de Fuca Strait,
> fingers reaching for someone in the dark.

Neighbours hose a patio
(their flow drawn from the lake)
clear underbrush and talk
in the giddy tones of newlyweds.

> Lake filling with winter freshets, with rain,
> draining through seasonal creeks and fissures,
> evaporating – then filling again.
> All the water we'll ever have is here.

A breeze lifts the shoreline's cedared veil,
ruffles the water's sateen sheen –
mirligoes of bright and shadow,
promises till death us do part.

FRAGRANT HARBOUR

the mountain stream surges like it wants to tell me everything,
the rain is spilling everything as well,
it's like one and a thousand spirits are vying to recount it all.

~ Liu Waitong,
Looking for Woodbrook Villa on Pokfulam Road

SAMPAN, 1962

This is not a sampan, it's a lullaby,
liquid song line in a viscous sea

thick with children, jellyfish boys
floating pale in warm moonlight,

bathing after a hot day
hawking plastic shoes.

This is not a boat, it's a woman:
bare feet deck-wedded, chest hard-pressed

into mahogany hands as she grips
a long sculling pole, rolls her burnished wrists.

Tonight she's steering for the Floating Palace,
restaurant pearled in strings of light.

Tanks of live fish: grouper, black bass,
small sharks prized for their fins.

Tanka rower plying these waters that bear
British names – Aberdeen, Stanley, Repulse Bay.

This passenger is not a little girl.
She is a broth steeped in the tang of otherness –

her expat family does not think they are wealthy;
the Tanka rower knows they are.

The girl swaying to the stern, asks if she can pole,
carve luminous the black sea

and the boatwoman allows,
clowns with such plumpness,

flashes a gap-toothed grin –
these gaps much larger than the girl imagines.

AFTER FIFTY YEARS,
RETURN TO HONG KONG

In the school entrance   small altar to history
snapshots of children who once played here

I peer at black and white photos
look for my face in the beanbag race

Quarry Bay Elementary   four years
tending a small garden in sub-tropical heat

learning netball and sums   enchanted
by a Welsh teacher reading of lions and wardrobes

The school now a Youth Centre   kindness remains
the director guides through old classrooms

still framed in polished wood   high ceilings
tall windows   the iron hook where I hung my
   cardigan

He photographs me by the bell tower
          background of scrub-clad hillsides remain

too steep for the builder's thumb
havens for wild pig   rare agarwood

and orchid trees   the highest peaks
still domes of red porphyry

I descend the one hundred and sixteen steps
to King's Road

an old man clasps his hands behind his bent back
to peer at shop displays   and I feel home

another language on buses   ·   Cantonese first then English
finally Mandarin   yet in schools this place *hoeng gong*

becomes *xiang gang*   the fight for what to keep
uncensored bookstores   unrestrained voice

the vote
          a yellow umbrella in case of rain

MAN O' WAR, 1963

Beyond the shark nets of Clearwater Bay,
in a cabin cruiser furnished with a captain,
the parents eat pigs in a blanket
while the kids cannonball off the bow,
or plunge like pearl divers
into the amniotic South China Sea,
pausing en route from stern to bow
for an icy Orange Spot, sticky and sweet
on blueing lips, or a fistful of salty crisps.
C'mon, c'mon, the kids call to the gods in the cockpit.
And the fathers stride marble and magnificent
to the bow before executing perfect jackknives.
The children froth around them,
wrapped in brief tentacles of paternity
before the fathers peel away,
and everyone clambers on board for another round.
My father launches first and comes up howling.
Portuguese man o' war, risen from below,
now at full sail, venomous tendrils billowing,
Dad yanking the swim ladder, water sliding
silver from his welted back. But he's laughing,
shouting for a towel, another scotch.

It is scarcity and plenty that make the vulgar take things
to be precious or worthless.
~ Sagredo, in *Galileo's Dialogues*

Mesmerized by diamonds spouting free from a drinking
fountain set in a bezel of cement, I pressed again the silver
button, bent to slurp and slurp from the silver tap. My
eye a loupe for sun-caught spray cut by July light. Brilliant
gems scattered along my tongue. I could not believe how
sweet, how free. Our family had flown home to Vancouver
that summer, flew everywhere guilt-free in the sixties.
The thirst for energy unquenched, we burned. The week
before, pale blue school shift pasted to my back, I'd
entered City Hall in Central District to ask for a glass
of water – no swigging from taps there, all water boiled,
poured into glass bottles, cooled. The woman at the
refreshment counter demanded five cents. Money for
water? Stunned, I dug into my pocket and gave what I'd
been saving to buy sweets from the hawker at the bus stop.
I'd never paid for water and they'd never charged, but this
was a time of drought – water shipped in tankers from
Mainland China. Water in homes only every four days;
every jug and both bathtubs filled. Those without tubs
lining at street taps for hours. *They call a diamond very
beautiful*, Sagredo says, *because it is like pure water, and
then would not exchange one for ten barrels of water*. In
Cantonese slang, the word water stands for money.
In the Causeway Bay district, jewellers sell diamonds for
many lumps of water.

They're hauling pear-shaped cuttlefish from the Pearl
River delta, snipping with big silver scissors, then
dropping the wide, white ribbons like rice noodles into
boiling cauldrons. Tai O, a Qing-dynasty fishing village
on the South China Sea, still disgorging perch, shrimp, and
croaker. I stroll the alleyways – jumble of homes, some
sheet metal, plywood, or brick tossed up the hill, others
perched on ironwood stilts above tidal flats, poised as
herons. Bits of corrugated roof, broken bicycles, buckets
with holes, parts of things no longer recognizable, pile like
hazy memories in mounds on empty lots. A young woman
in faded blue cotton squats and rinses *gai lan* – bright
green in a silver bowl – and later, while the vegetables
drip in a colander, she swishes a pink slab of liver.

mahjong game in a room
I stop in the lane to watch
the door close

Solid as legend, a Ming-era temple to Kwan Tai
(a general renowned for loyalty) surveys a public square.
Hard Hill roof style, curved tiles in slate gray and glazed
turquoise. Under the shade of a banyan tree, blue, white,
and jade-green gods gambol along the roof ridge. Inside,
an old man tends the smoke of incense, of stargazer lilies
perfuming the small rooms. I make a donation; the
proffered oranges of believers glow in candlelight. Just
beyond the square, young people, wearing masks to hide
their faces, congregate at the bus stop. Headed for pro-
democracy demonstrations in the city centre. Restless
in the lineup.

mists caught in old hills
from the protests for freedom
a tattered banner

They have built what is, for now, the longest open-sea fixed link in the world. The Hong Kong-Zhuhai-Macau Bridge launches from this old fishing village, crosses the Pearl River delta. Hunger roars in the back alleys of blood, hawkers hustle, a child nudges another to capture a rolling ball. I board a metal boat. Salt and wind buff my cheek as the skiff whizzes beyond the harbour so I can view the bridge, search for pink dolphins.

white crane lifts from mudflats
gray bridge and soaring cables
span two worlds

Embroidered napkin. Junk in cross-stitch
red flag, blue sail, brown crescent hull
afloat on a white-cotton sea,
trimmed with pink lilies.
No stink of pig or diesel,
no cooking grease, no
crowded family voices insistent as rain
stain this cloth. No lamp-fishing applique –
dull whomp of moonlit dynamite,
sudden scoop of stunned silver – no
rooster crow at dawn done in crewel wool.
Did the stitcher imagine someone like me
daubing lips, red blush from the plum sauce
of our cook's sweet and sour fish?
She wouldn't know about the day
I swam into a dead pig
fallen overboard in Lo Lo Shing,
my hand thunking hard
on its fly-embroidered eye.

My parents welcome the guests.
Your wrap? A drink?
I offer platters of small chow

concocted by our cook from the pages
of English entertainment guides –
Plumrose sausage speared

with blue cocktail picks
bite-sized pastries, shrimp chips.
Small chow, what they called these party snacks,

and my ten-year-old eyes
have seen a small Chow dog
de-furred and pickled, curled

like a foetus in a large glass jar
in Stanley Village – blanched peach
afloat in amber syrup.

Dressed in crinolines
and pink gingham in summer,
plum velvet in winter,

or dipped in plaid in the fall,
I play party games with the guests,
three-dimensional Xs and Os –

three Plexiglas sheets with holes,
stacked equidistant on four silver legs.
This night I am the blue pegs,

the Danish diplomat, the red.
We play beside the marble fireplace,
trying to form unbroken lines.

I beat him just as my mother
strolls over brandishing a platter,
a flutter of napkins.

Who won? she asks.
I did, says the diplomat.
        Small chow anyone?

1966, aerial photograph:
airport runway extended into the sea

> *landing at Kai Tak*
> *apartment windows rattle –*
> *a duck glides on water*

Section 6.4, government report
shelter for boat people paramount

> *sea gypsy child*
> *after centuries afloat*
> *a school bell*

Plate 6.11, the coastline changes
reclamation of the sea

> *mainland refugees*
> *move from shack to high rise –*
> *fragrant harbouring*

Section 2.2, Gin Drinkers Bay filled
with Kowloon refuse: Lap Shap Wan (Rubbish Bay)

> *children play*
> *on the field at Kwai Fong –*
> *what do the worms eat?*

Section 2.1, 1961, 3.1 million
100,000 persons a month from China

> *eight million people –*
> *in the packed subway tonight*
> *close scent of camphor*

Mother smokes Rothman's,
writes letters from her escritoire –
drop leaf, camphor wood, and carved,
the four winds blowing from each foot.

A man sings the Crocodile Shirt jingle
on the radio in English
with a strong Cantonese accent:
Comfo[r]t, E[l]regance, Qua[l]rity ...

On this far side of the island, my sister and I
mock the accent from our gilded perch,
(elegance, sounding a lot like arrogance)
in our spacious apartment overlooking the sea.

Comfot, Eregance, Quarity, repeat.
Always look for C[r]ocodile,
C[r]ocodile it sui[t]s you well,
Always look for C[r]ocodile

Then a female voice floats in: *of Cou[r]se.*
And the man joins her
for a spirited crescendo of:
C[r]ocodile S[h]iiiirt!

I sing as I stroke the yellow canary
before cleaning her cage on the balcony,
pour seeds from one hand to another,
sifting, blowing the husks out to sea.

Mother writes home about the parties,
the business trips with father.
(Comfort. Elegance. Quality.)
Oh, and the girls. *Always look for ...*

Tonight my mother will wear
the pink silk with beaded bodice.
I will shrug off her kiss to make her pay,
just a little, for yet another leave-taking.

I fill with fresh seeds and croon to the canary.
Was this the day I left the cage door open?
How soon did the freedom I thought a gift
fill a hawk's beak?

Cherry Silk: The Master

It's spring and I want to paint peaches
but first, a dish of lychees, a sip of tea,
and this commission for Governor Wu,
    a lover of black bamboo in snow.

Drop the jade weights
on the corners of practice sheets –
elm bark and polished rice –
    save the white silk for good.

Chilly this morning. I curve palms around cup,
then warm up with a few quick strokes.
The ink thick as blood,
    my wrist a bit stiff.

A scene from the poet
Wang will do nicely –
his lilts and twists
    in Farm Garden Happiness, no. 4:

Spring grass is green, luxuriant, and fragrant;
pines cold but kind, strong with gentleness.
Cows and sheep return at dusk down village pathways.
Children can't distinguish the governor by hat or dress.

That should get him thinking!
Pines, of course, a bridge, a shadow of mountain.
What did the Masters see? I'll add
    peach blossom on a branch.

Press, lift, glide, press –
the branch, a bone.
Dot, swirl, a knuckle
    where bough bursts from trunk.

The colour cakes are dry,
hollowed in the centre,
but just enough pink
    for a turn of blossom.

Cherry silk for the scroll.
Mei Li! Exquisite!
Have it delivered by Wednesday …
    My tea is cold. Where is my man?

Ink Stick: The Servant

Ai ya! This house on the Peak is cold
in the mornings. The mists drift past the veranda,
catch in the pines, like the scrolls of the old masters.
    I make tea first – sepia oolong,

a dish of lychees,
peeled for my master
who rises late. My slippers slap
    the parquet floors. Hiss

of the kettle, *fai-dee-la*, hurry, hurry
scoop leaves into the celadon pot. My master likes
the wolf-tail brushes with bamboo stems
 lined from fat to slim, each cupped in its ivory stand.

Pine-soot ink sticks, hard and black
and I take one, add small water –
he'll hit me, the old rooster,
 if I don't get it right –

For forty years I've dipped in a shallow dish
ground in a clockwise motion –
ai ya, how my elbows have ached –
 until the liquid turned a viscous black.

For forty years, lids lifted from colour pots –
yellow for the umber of sparrows on snow,
a touch of blue in spring leaves,
 carmine for peach blossoms, watered to pink.

Brushstroke: The Master

His father was my father's man,
and our hair grows grey together
like the wash of ink on rice paper,
 the slow light of dusk.

I hear the scuff of his slippers,
watch as he pours my tea.
I know he watches me.
 I lift my brush, plump it with ink,

raise my arm,
hand poised
like a heron
    I strike

the unfurled sheet,
a lift, a glide, another press –
turtledove calling for rain,
    crane among clouds ...

Back in the kitchen, he strikes garlic
with the side of his cleaver,
puts the point to the block,
    presses.

Rice Paper: The Servant

Sometimes in the night I take
a sheet of good rice paper,
lay its polished whiteness
    on my new-swept floor

let my son
trace a tree with a dry brush –
one of my master's seconds.
    I notice how the boy

feathers the leaf tip
a little longer than master,
how he gives the blossom
    an extra turn.

I keep the brush;
the paper I return
each morning –
    my son's lines barely visible.

LIKE A MOTH TO A FLAME

> Classes struggle, some classes triumph, others are
> eliminated. Such is history.
> ~ Mao Tse-tung, "The Little Red Book"

After a night of struggle
in the bright of a Coleman lamp,
I find you dead in the morning –

wings a light green leaf,
black shroud
crosshatched on a singed thorax.

Moth, swirling above my head
last night as I lay on the porch
in my summer bed. You rested,

for a moment, punch-drunk,
felt safe in the harbour
my hipbone held for you.

I was reading a history of Hong Kong –
Communist-led riots in a fight
against colonial Britain.

Tiny bugs assaulted
the white heat above my head.
dropped, died on my chest

on the "6" of 1926, the "o" of offences
of British rule, the "u" of unionists arrested,
staining the white page. In the end,

a rout, yet only important Communists
protected by the Party, the rest left
to be shipped to Nationalist China,

to torture or death. Believers
burned in a confused clash with fire,
upward launch toward reflected light,

despite its untrue moon, its false dawn.
And here you are, moth, dead in the morning.
Dead to the woodpecker's hollow knock.

I place you on a spider's web,
woven script between railings,
softest of unheralded graves.

HIKE ON LANTAU ISLAND, 1968

Teenage girls   we climb
to the peak of Lantau's mountain

the path narrow   deep-worn
dust and dried plum salty in our mouths

scrub pine
all afternoon

we trail
under a sun

huge and adamant
as any Empire

this   old   landscape
chiaroscuro

painted by the Masters
with scrupulous strokes

wet brush   black ink
washed and veiled

dry brush   dark green
quick flicks   needles

Mary Hopkin's top of the pops
Those were the days my friends

we sing loud and happy
like Li Bai drunk under the moon.

Once set on white linen,
lifted by my mother's slim fingers,
polished nails, and shaken
just the once, its high glitter-ring
      and the servant comes,
Ah Lee in his starched white jacket,
knotted frog buttons, pressed black pants,
comes running with another celadon bowl
steaming, a silver ladle;
or his wife Ying comes with a question,
Yes, missy, you wanji something? Small golden bell
carved as the temple roofs at Angkor Wat,
domed as a straw bee hive, loop handle at its top,
bought in a market in Bombay,
brought to her table on an island
in the South China Sea. This bell nestled among other
objects of wealth – candle-snuffer
with ivory cup, silver table-crumb remover,
cement servant-quarters. She had trouble
ringing it at first, my mother,
but she got used to it.
      Got used to the cocktail parties, the thousand
        dinners out
in apartments overlooking the Fragrant Harbour,
all built on the back of this bell, its Pavlovian ring.
This bell now withdrawn to a middle-class nation,
sits dull-coated in kitchen grease,
dirt-grooved, tarnished
on a white window sill, silent.

EIGHT IMITATIONS
OF THE POET WANG WEI

Li-yang River

On Hong Kong's Peak, camphor and mulberry trees.
The city below sprouts pink and white stone –
my childhood home of seven years, its
fragrant harbour now obscured by Shenzhen smudge.
In the distance, the South China Sea
floods into the harbour's arms. It's the year 2017 CE
Do they embrace or shield for attack?
Both – *judging from talk in the marketplace.*

Returning to Wang–chu'an

Tai Tam reservoir, scene of family picnics.
Corrugated orange cliffs ring celadon water.
I'm strolling memory's bridges –
my parents, grandfather, aunts, once vivid
along these paths, now withered grass.
Ferns, shrubs, the Bamboo-leaf oak
paint the hills dark jade, dull silver.
As I climb the bus steps, *grief seizes.*

Splendid Day on the River Han

At the Orange Peel café poets converge;
words splash beyond earth and sky.
A reader morphs into a Blue tiger butterfly.
We flit to bars lit by a thousand moons.
Ah, what a splendid night
to get reeling drunk
　　　with the poets of Soho!

At Hsin-yi Hamlet

Crossing Des Voeux Road, Tuesday lunchtime.
Bright hibiscus of a woman: high heels,
black skirt, red blouse. Her petal face
tilted to spring sun, a young man slim, dark-suited
beside her. They laugh in English and Cantonese.
If I'd stayed, would I have been her?
The vine still blooms and falls, still blooms and falls.

Hsiang-chi Monastery

As pilgrim to the treasure cave of pirate Cheung Po Tsai,
I pass Bun Tower scaffolds in Taoist (now tourist)
festival preparation for young men to scale in May,
pass two grandfathers bent to a game of croquet..Here
on Cheung Chau island I climb cliffs
where *waters moan against the perilous rocks*
to the pirate cave, its entrance
narrow as my outstretched arm. Tucked in a crevice,
a merchant sells key chains, sacred plastic figurines –
no *meditation drives the virulent dragon from the heart.*
No. Here commerce drives hunger from the belly.

Farm Garden Happiness, no. 7

Along the waterfront at Sai Kung,
yellow acacia blossoms against a purple March sky.
Blue skiffs crammed with crab, sea bream.
Purse-seiners, trawlers scrape the reefs.
I scoop shrimp and sea urchin
into my limpet mouth. At the indoor market,
three youths sell organic pork,
cutlets they've raised from a Bristol pig.

Lake Yi

At the end of Station Lane, a tiny garage,
damp walls festooned with tarnished tools.
Riots for freedom flood the streets, yet
the owner darts, dragonfly chasing bugs,
beneath, above, beside a Mercedes
squeezed into his shop. Every inch jammed,
but in a corner, a shrine: Choi San, military god
of wealth, electric-lit and fêted – gold bullfrog
bolstering the long night of labour.

You Come from My Hometown

You come from my hometown and must recall
Dragon's Back, climbing its granite spine.
Tell me, do the winds from east and west
thrill you, almost knock you flat?

GENE POOL

Any little thing is water.

~ Gertrude Stein, *Tender Buttons*

POOLS

On business trips, my father took photos of pools.
Kidney-shaped, rectangular, oval.
Palm-fringed, vine-draped,
or wending like a river under bougainvillea.

On his return he clicked transparencies
into his slide projector,
beamed pools onto a screen.
Turquoise, aquamarine, night-lit sapphire.

Dipped, his heavy body felt light.
Liquid heft floating his withered leg
shrivelled from childhood.
Pools closed to him during the polio scare –

mothers pulling their children
from public waters.
Who knows how he got sick,
how he survived?

Each time he donned Hawaiian-print trunks,
a baptismal plunge: layers of cool possibility,
legs and arms
        scrawling the blank page of water.

CROSSWORD

1 Across: circles back to the thrower (9 letters)

Returned from a great distance, you curve
over the crossword at the kitchen table.
Daughter-moved-back-home,
your new phrase for yourself. You wear

your setbacks like an afternoon housecoat
while we search for the right word.
This time, you're not alone. You bring
a man and a dog. We always wanted

a large family. Your old room a puzzle of boxes.
In the kitchen, light seeps through windows
melting with rain. We slip clementines
from their skins and fill in the blanks.

2 Down: success in a struggle (7 letters)

The fry pan you used for dinner last night
clogs my resolve for smooth sailing.
Cooked egg whites float, foam
in a greasy sea. Do I speak up?

We're all glad your younger mother
isn't here anymore, the one who lost
her battle with impatience, who missed
the clue: if you can't say anything nice ...

and sure enough, by afternoon, and without
words, even the compost tin, emptied and rinsed,
dries triumphantly on the countertop –
its silver lid, a polished medal.

3 Across: *deep feeling of affection (4 letters)*

Tonight we crowd into your bedroom,
perch on the pullout,
swap stories of your new jobs,
your short trip away.

We are bone-carved
in the same tribal pattern. You, tossed
from our hold, flying
your elliptical path. Tell me,

in that book you are reading, does the daughter's hair
shine under a yellow lamp, and her lover sing
while waltzing through rooms? Does the father
smooth his travelled hand along the mother's cheek?

BURNT POT, RIVERBANK, INDIFFERENT SKY

Liz, next door to my old aunt,
phones and says Aunt Claire gets lost,
drives through red lights, burns pots.
That first night I arrive,
her house far from town,
my aunt thinks the best way
to shut me up
on care homes is to state plain
in words of one syll-a-ble
what she wants.

She's a wild goat   my childless aunt
coarse salt and silver-wire hair
invisible horns saddling a face
braving confusion's squall
insisting on her   moon-life
monastic home far from town
on the sage banks of a wide flood,
full of the snow's melt.

She pats her black and white cat
who is so fat his gut strokes the floor,
says, *I want to die here with Bear.*
That's what I want, she says,
even though they say I can't drive,
nor tell time, nor thread a maze
on that dumb test they gave me.

I'll try and make it so, I say,
I'll try.

Fall and we stroll the riverbank to view stunned salmon
clotting the shores, their rock-flensed flesh in patches.

White head dipped in winter light,
she jams shapes into a jigsaw puzzle.
The small pieces are difficult to fit.
But nothing, she says, *a hammer won't fix.*
Some days we pick plums from her trees,
pesky mushrooms from her matted lawn.

She taught me to swim in Shuswap Lake, auntie who asks
    me every week
where I'm calling from. Who says: *I'm afraid I'll forget
    who you are.*
Her hands below my spine holding me in the lake,
    swirling loose limbs, making water friendly.

Ruminant icon of my mother
their wild dove days
her   wild pear heart
stone-still over a child's shape-shifting puzzle
ghosts of oil lamps   sometimes honey suckle
sometimes braided rug
unwoven mind butting against small bridges
the always-river she's lived beside.

Walking the river beneath Russian Olive trees,
we greet a warden repairing a tumbled bridge.
Aunt bends to mud, lugging boulders to help.
Lure of activity always pulling.
She grunts, heaves chunks of rock
into the wire mesh frame he's built
to patch the small bridge. My skeletal aunt
deep-knees another stone into the scaffold,
absurd hold against an always-crumbling bank.

I'm afraid I'll forget who you are, she says.
But we won't forget you, I reply.
Where do you live? she asks and I tell her. Ask
about the birds she feeds with suet. *You live
in the moment*, I say. *You're becoming
a Buddhist. Yeah*, she laughs, *that's it.*

Her run not yet up, she scorns
the bleached bones of depleted salmon.
And I wonder: why not mud-caked and struggling
die hefting your fateful boulder toward an indifferent sky?

Where are you calling from?
And every time the answer is the same: from far away.
   From further away
each time I call as she sinks deeper and deeper and I have
   no hands to hold her –

the name of her dead husband
my name   fallen Russian olives   ruined plums.

I PAY A MAN TO WASH THE WINDOWS

Clive climbs the silver ladder to the clerestory windows
we've added since last year. He doesn't charge more.

He borrows a white bucket, dish soap; has his own squeegee
    and rag,
tells me he learned the trade from a baker in Chinatown

who cracked a broom handle in half for the squimjim
and gave him his first job on the bakery front.

It's a job I could do, have done many times of a sunny
    afternoon,
but he does it better, maybe needs the work.

Clive hoses my windows, coats them in soapy water, carves
his rubber blade in clean lines: dolphins curving in sudsy
    waves.

My aunt's voice, a summer bee caught indoors,
caroms around the kitchen as I busy myself

with a stock pot – marrow bone, carrots, celery –
she'd never pay to have another do her work.

The house sighs, shivers with pleasure,
a finger stroking its backbone.

HOW WE NAME THINGS FROM
OUR OWN SEAT IN THE CHEVY

Commonly called a Smoker's Window,
or No Draft, the vent,
a small triangle in glass
(tucked where the window
met the dash in the front
or the trunk in the rear)
found in old Studebakers,
Chevys, and Fords.
As a small child I'd stick my nose
out the vent to clear
the Rothmans or Players
from pink-sponge lungs,
to subvert a tendency
to car-sickness; for years,
convinced the intimate window
was called a Nose Draft,
my personal escape hatch
from hours of Sunday looky-looing
(mother's time to get out of the house)
the window custom-built for my need.
        My fly-me-to-the-moon father,
butterscotch scent of aftershave and glory,
taught me at sixteen to drive.
The Nose Draft is stuck,
I said to him one lesson day,
The what?

ON TAMING FOXES

Tu deviens responsable pour toujours de ce que
tu as apprivoisé.
~ Antoine de Saint-Exupéry, *Le Petit Prince*

It's a Saturday morning when you run away
to the orphanage down the street,
dad flipping pancakes. You're not quite seven
and furious at your older sister's desecration
of Shaggy, beloved blue stuffed pet,
and at your parent's cool rebuke, or
were you sensing the unfairness
of how your world leashed a girl?
      The biology of tameness is elusive;
though they've found a phenotype for friendliness.
Siberian foxes bred for forty years
(piebald coats, floppy ears) will leap as kits
into their master's arms, lick human cheeks,
whine when left alone in cages.
      Nobody comes to fetch you,
and the orphanage steps are cold.
They've kept a stack of jacks warm –
maple syrup, a bowl of strawberries.
Your sister slides the syrup in your direction.
The foxes have even begun to wag their tails.

PIERCED

It must have been a weekday for the workmen to be there.
Sleeves rolled, arms bare. I'm six, skipping in the vacant lot
next door, playing with pals when my cry and crumple
bring him striding across the buckled humps of dirt.
I've known his kindness to the kids through the weeks
he's been building a new house. This thrill at seeing him.
A yearning already kneading my unbaked heart.
The young man with dark curls kneels
to see the nail lodged in the pad of my foot,
the rusty blood. He swings me up, whisks me home
to the family's small bathroom with the yellow curtains
and crowds it with my mother who has hurried
with her auburn hair, clutching
Mercurochrome in a midnight-blue bottle. I'm perched
on the edge of the sink, gripping my mother's neck.
The young man croons in Portuguese
while water slides from cool to warm.
Plaster speckles the dark silk of his forearms,
the tanned back of his broad hands
working with my mother's polished pink fingertips
to remove the nail, daub disinfectant.
A warm breeze shyly lifts the curtain's hem
as blood sluices bright from my small foot,
pierced and resting
on the white sheet of porcelain.

SLANT RHYME FOR ORCHID

Well heaven forgive him! and forgive us all!
~ W. Shakespeare, *Measure for Measure*

Painted in the celadon bowl's heart –
blue figures taking tea. Took me
hours to find. Antique market
in Kurashiki where everything
seemed to echo of old isolation.
I loved the bowl at first sight,
but left it to steep before buying.
Found amber and golden teacups,
cobalt blue hairpins for courtesan coils.
But always returned to this soup bowl,
thick-sided daily ware.
Its cost politely negotiated, its safety
wrapped in newspapers and soft clothes,
the bowl arrived pristine to my kitchen.
At mealtimes the bowl
holds miso and rice,
murmurs orchids and wind chimes.
My husband comes to me this morning,
confesses in a low voice,
proffers the damaged offering.
His love of the dishwasher,
pride of hasty loading. What's a slant rhyme
for orchid? I stare at the chip on the porcelain rim –
white flaw beneath glossy green – ah yes,
late snowflake on a spring paddy.

Ah, Icarus, you always loved
the hum of the kick wheel
at the village kiln back on Crete,
its earthy business, the feathering of clay.
The cup our local potter helped you make,
red ribbons of coiled feldspar,
I fill with whatever is in bloom –
buttercup, field lace, wild purple lupin.
But your father had other plans.
Disdained the craftsmen,
tethered to their dirt,
their slow and patient flight
toward invention.
And then the news.
        I know what they say, and I know it's not true:
                not in pride you flew too high, but in pleasing.
Your broken father called me to Sicily.
Most evenings I find him drunk
and staring at the kilns
fired all night by sweat-glazed men.
Days he squats by their workshop,
deaf to the villagers, their many-cornered whispers,
as he watches the potters shave chips of clay
from plume-shaped vases and dip
trimmed feet in vats of boiling wax.

GRANDDAUGHTER IN ANOTHER CITY

If I were to write about you
I'd say   longing
palpable as water.

Since you were born
something weighty
as the family Lab thudding a welcome
into my thigh. I would tell you

how we waited for you
to travel like starlight
from the amniotic sky.

If I were to say completion,
I might come near
to how you snugged
into my enrobed chest,
my heritage-apple breasts
remembering.

If   surprise
at how my veins sizzled
when I saw your photograph today –

virtual you smiling
crackling air,
the ocean between us.

BACKYARD

The two girls next door join me to halt the mint
from its spread in the corner beds –
a good idea gone bad. We yank
tentacled roots, transplant to a pot for their mother.

All afternoon, spring mud cold
on Lily's toes but she refuses shoes,
skips between garden fork and trowel,
seed drill, and hand rake.

Isla harvests dandelion leaves,
makes homes for worms,
graves for grubs –
earth soaking Lily's toes, Isla's fingertips.

I dig as my elders before me –
mother, grandmothers, and aunts
in rhubarb patch, for English pea,
raspberry, potato, and spinach.

Generations bent over earthen beds –
my sister's beefsteak tomatoes
thick-cut on buttered bread
a sprinkle of salt, of evening sun

through the kitchen window.
What would these women have done
without a garden to dig troubles deep,
turn grievance to green bean?

In the housing density discussions
single-family dwellings are shameful –
what everyone wants but can no longer afford –
backyards paved for parking.

Will neighbours in a condo
put down roots from balconies?
Will they know when I've fallen?
Visit with buttercups?

A Mother's Day memory, hot sun and family
lunched and stunned in our backyard. My son
turns on the sprinkler for the kids, teaches
his apartment-dwelling toddler this new word.

At the base of the old chestnut
I build a fairy house with my grandchild –
unicorns in porcelain, painted doorway,
polished stone path.

When the townhouse or condo kids come,
tentative as ungulates, or bold as crows,
I'll invite them to my backyard
offer them trowels, a nickel a weed.

Five o'clock by the time the girls and I gather
our clutch of mint, steep leaves to tea,
drink pale green from china cups.
We nibble cookies by the window overlooking

the flowerbeds, vegetable plots, grounding grass.
Their father joins me for a glass of wine
and the restless children go outside,
dig heels in un-trafficked turf, run and run.

BABY IN THE BATHWATER

~ for GK

Fizzle and pip-zip, this toddler
granddaughter on multi-coloured mats,
in toy houses and sand,
hula-hooping the day
all the way to this bath soaking
her plush skin and I am tear-free
shampoo, soft cloth, remembering
my high-school biology teacher
telling the class not to have children
(too many people fructifying like fruit flies)
Malthus sounding death knells, then *Silent Spring*
(too many chemicals). *How could you?*
someone asked of my pregnancy,
the early eighties so futureless,
my body swelling under flowered prints.
I'd chosen life.
Look how she folds her body into mine –
eggshell human, albumen
running from her nose
disease-vector, heart-swooper,
freighted with who we are,
want to be. How we waited for her
to arrive from the Long Night moon
in a waxing crescent.
Now squeeze the yellow ducky,
her accordion laugh,
dissuade her gulps of sudsy, city water

(not worried about the suds)
fill a pink cup to stream over fine hair,
slope of new shoulders, her two belly pleats
and I am apples from the backyard tree,
kale from my garden.
Her buoyant will gushes, spills,
strong-fisted thwacking,
delight of displacement and drench.
        Some say we are a tribe of the land-sick lost
floating at the end of the world. Still
we have peek-a-boo with the yellow cloth,
and this afternoon's Monarch –
its milkweed wings dipping
in a river of white roses –
her own flight of discovery.
        And now after the bath
wrapped in thick flannel,
her eyes drift closed
        confident in the coming of

CHANGING

~ *for* HQ

Most times I know when to change
your diaper. Note the sudden stop
in your toddle, the soft grunt, glistening eyes
after waking, after meals.
Nothing your body produces fazes me.
I remember to clasp ankles,
truss them in my fingers.
Muscle memory in the swift lift,
in how to hold my breath.

Your father and your aunt
as small children
snuck into my mother's purse once
and opened the paper carton,
broke all her Rothmans,
so my parents quit.
I take more trips to exercise class.
Lift weights for you.

Before the final wrap, I pucker and blow
on your clean belly,
explosions of pressed air,
squeeze from a tiny chest
and the world locks into place –
just you and me
my historic hands bracing
your unblemished torso,
            lips to belly, that laugh. Repeat.

ON FRIDAYS WITH YOU, THIS GAME

When you first yanked down
your baby blanket of peek-a-boo

how we all loved knowing
you were inside your wordlessness

too soon, you,
at eighteen months,

switch to a quick flick of one hand
before your face, a rapid fling –

abbreviated, as if you'd had enough.
How can I already be missing

our game to say:
we'll find each other?

RECIPE WITH EGGS

In a blue bowl, we crack eggs. Pastel brown, pliant.
Not able to break. Me neither. Crack, yes. One two three
and more. Tiny tap cracks. Plunge thumbs and the
   supple shell.
You want to do everything by yourself, with me.
I want to do everything by yourself with you, small
   granddaughter.
After a shower I bend forward, you ask, then pat my
   bare breasts.
You'll have these, too. We smile.
Something to do with the body. The eggs I've shed,
   fertilized,
killed. Slippery whites run under shirt cuffs. Roll up
   the sleeves.
Crack another, then another. Splash milk. Pour oil
   in the fry pan.
Whisk, whisk.

Colour of spittle, colour of catamenia.
Skinny dipping, held and floating free.
Paradise of present. Silken unknowing.
Glycerin-self forming intentions
in bone chips, gold flakes, veined water.
Pain, yes. Coffee? Maybe. Also taste of honey.
Voices through a scrim of gushing.
Blind heartbeat rooting through nerves.
Cacophony of scat as cells proliferate
under shadowy panes. Bunkered greenhouse.
Wet walls finely touched, the cord. Automatic sprinkler
temperature of blood, of the southern Pacific.
Growth and growth until water rents
in plashes of burning air.

WHAT WATER WANTS

Water is God's wine, and there is no more.

~ Anonymous

EVE RIVER ESTUARY

The river is thick with whale-herded salmon.
An eagle scoops bright Coho, slow swoops
its cargo low into the sheltering green.
I fish from estuary banks stitched in sea grass.

An eagle scoops bright Coho, slow swoops.
My arm sweeps up, wrist flicks.
I fish from estuary banks stitched in sea grass.
Bite of a Silver and the line glint-whips.

My arm sweeps up, wrist flicks –
leaping fish, life-lit. Its shine and struggle.
Silver bite and the line glint-whips.
I beach its death on a stone altar,

this leaping fish, life-lit, its shine and struggle.
I drop a heavy rock, still its foil eye,
beach its death on a stone, alter
everything in the slice of a gutting knife

hard as a dropped rock, a foiled eye.
Stroke its glossy belly and slit clean.
Slice with a gutting knife,
cut free the gill, plum-red fan.

Stroke its glossy belly and slit clean,
spill milt sacs smooth as custard,
cut free the gill, plum-red fan,
grate thumbnail along the spine's ridge.

Look! Spilt milt sacs smooth as custard,
this male's procreative silk.
Grate thumbnail along the spine's ridge,
loose the jellied blood and sluice

this male's procreative silk.
Tug out his finned heart.
Loose the jellied blood and sluice
into our shared river

his tugged heart.
Watch the blood strands stream
into our shared river,
spin out with the sighing tide.

Watch a blood strand stream
its cargo low into the sheltering green,
spin out with the sighing tide
to a sea once thick with whale and salmon.

WITH NO SWEET WATER
水调歌头·难溯甘泉

After Li Xinmo's photographs "The Death of Xinkai River,"
with translation by Liu Xia and Tang Haiyue

i

What would the ancient poets say of poisoned Xinkai river?
Wang Wei and Li Bai exiled on state business,
> wine-drunk and swapping lines beside a green stream.

毒淖几曾有？太白问摩诘。

We know poison, they might say, as when Empress Wei
fouled her husband's veins to put her son on the throne.
> We know fire ships, blazing rivers in the time of
> > Warring States.

却道韦氏帝梦，战火连营间。

But burning rivers marked a time of war, though perhaps,
it is always a time of war. We know the Emperors of greed,
> their creeping slaughter of the river-huddled peasant.

太平盛世如梦，又添百姓疾苦，何处无民怨。

Pass the jug, they might shout,
with no sweet water,
> exile.

辗转过山岳，此世无甘泉。

Black-haired girl in a white shift, her back to the lens,
belly down, face partially submerged.
How to love a stinging stream? Photograph yourself in it.
素衣白，青丝黛，沉朱颜。
Blue-green algae petals her bare shoulders.
Dead-woman river; dark-hair weeds,
close-up skin lined in burning rills.
青荇缠绕，玉陨冰肌江水燃。
How to recover from phosphorous, nitrogen?
River as waste. Septic
waterway unfurls to the sea.

Xin, meaning New. Kai, Open.
Newly Opened River now closed.
Condos and factories its riparian zone.
浊水又见新居。
Blue-green algae born from the dark,
viridian pearls lacing the dead woman's hand. Witness
in the click of a shutter.
快门闪过人言，

The river is weary. A muddy green
thickens its once-shimmering blood.
　　The willow no longer strokes its back.

The men fishing from the mound
fertile with apricot trees are ghostly shadows.
　　Imperial officials hold high meetings
　　树影惊魍魉。
while Xinkai hurts for the white-nosed sturgeon
Ah, its cool-moon body,
　　the rustle and tickle of fin.
　　新开河上冷，华堂声正喧。

水调歌头·难溯甘泉
毒淖几曾有？太白问摩诘。却道韦氏帝梦，战火连营间。
太平盛世如梦，又添百姓疾苦，何处无民怨。辗转过山
岳，此世无甘泉。素衣白，青丝黛，沉朱颜。青荇缠绕，
玉陨冰肌江水燃。浊水又见新居，快门闪过人言，树影惊
魍魉。新开河上冷，华堂声正喧。

Hazel, the park warden, lets rain drip from her nose,
and wind fling the drops as she talks above the panting
volcano. She whips out plastic-wrapped photos from
the 1800s, the 1950s, and this recent eruption of people
edging close to fire, to earth shattering and forming. A
photo of a golfer mid-swing, Kilauea billowing cloud and
ash and lava bombs behind him. *Always go for adventure*,
Hazel laughs. She loves this weather. Hard rain batters,
and she calls us tourists brave, says, *Never be afraid.*

How things came here: wind, water, and wings. Wind-
blown seeds, ocean currents carrying a floating coconut.
And birds, their berry droppings taking hold: in porous
black lava, sudden green. Hazel pauses to galvanize our
group around the native fiddleheads, slender purple stalks
spiralling at the top. Then veers from the path to a crack
in the earth. Steam flares from fathoms below. We lean.
Hot gusts poach pores. Wind and rain and steam.

Did you know the ohia tree, she says, *is from the same
myrtle plant native to Texas?* Birds and seeds. We reach
the sulphur banks. Rotten egg smell, yellow smears and
white crystals, drifts of vapour. Drifts of amber grass
clutch life, take slow control. We perch on a bridge, see
dinosaurs grazing. *This will be green again*, Hazel says,
long after we're gone.

And Hawaii Island will slide off its ocean hotspot as
Oahu has, as Maui has. Another volcano growing even
now beneath the sea will emerge, spill more land and
the continents will crash back together, swallowing the
Pacific. *Cycles*, says Hazel. *Cycles*. We stand reverential
in this change. Wonder at our place in it.
We'd like to stay.

How things come here: the three Ws – wind, water, wings.
And some add a fourth, says Hazel:
Walmart.

Winter is dark but blue walls of light
are everywhere – networks we wade through,
wireless bead curtains, hum.

Domestic nets flow faint,
cluster like moon jellies,
          waterfall silver from apartment windows.

Office signals shower streets,
envelop parks. No unlit corner left.
          Believe this:

we're simmering in immaterials.
Put an ear to the falling snow,
          hear it stroke the mesh, carol like glass harps.

ARGUMENT WITH CAPTAIN VANCOUVER
OVER THE NAMING OF DESOLATION SOUND

Let's say you had good reason –
take that afternoon in August
I saw a gull swallow a starfish.
Each purple finger sinking
slowly into the sea-bird's bitter sea.
All afternoon I watched
as the Pacific lapped the hull,
sun the sandstone. The gull
agape, anchored in its terrible song,
the sea star taking its little steps
down to ruin.

— * —

You, Captain, the once-rising star,
slow-swallowed by a hierarchy back home,
mad with illness, whipping your way north:
Willm. Wooderson, Seaman: 24 lashes for Insolence;
John Thomas: 36 Lashes for Neglect of Duty.

— * —

I sail to Desolation,
wind lashing my cheek,
clouds flaring above the tilting cliffs.

I paddle in coves beneath pictographs
of red ochre fish and their drying racks.

— * —

Reek of rot and sweat. June night *Discovery*
enters the Sound, winds light and fluky,
a coastal drizzle and a serpentine tide.
Maze of blue islands and inlets
smudged with fir and pine.
Blindfolded, you said, *in this labyrinth*.

Lost in your black maze, you launched long boats
like water beetles to survey.
You turned to astronomy. Trusted lunars
to show where you were.

— * —

I find my bearings by clouds of moon jellies
afloat beneath my anchored boat,
pulsing the sea's bright night,
their milky way, unfurling.

— * —

We can all do it: name from our own sad story.
Desolate, you float away,
having christened and claimed,
done your duty by King George.
Hold piled with pelts, masks, clubs, and traces
of the nights the crewmen traded
their pewter plates for time
with the women of the Sound.

What must the women of the Sound have said?

— * —

Rolled and stored, your painstaking charts
now guide tankers to these ship-swallowing shores,
and cracked hulls threaten
to cloak ducks in black satin.

Your lament:

Our residence here was truly forlorn;
an awful silence pervaded the gloomy forests,
whilst animated nature seemed to have deserted.

Perhaps you were a seer, after all.

And who am I? Sheathed in petroleum fleece,
warmed by a sailboat's ticking diesel heat.

— * —

Moon jellies care nothing for our desolation.
Small bells, illumed by shafts of salty light,
sound in my sternum a deep tuning.

— * —

In Desolation Sound sage and silver mosses
drip from summer-brown cliffs, pink arbutus
unpeels its skin, evergreens fur the air sweet
and I plunge into a warm sea.

Some days, rain drums the deck,
tumbles through channels, beads
bright as mercury on the crazed-glass hatch
slips otter-like overboard.
Rain all day, erodes, loosens
the self, kelp whip fluttering on a wave.

— * —

I know we have to fumble
for direction, descriptors –
some with history's wounds
bruising just beneath –

but here,
let's glide with the governing tide.
    Listen! How sea purls sibilant on stone,
    names itself, sounds its own.

Five dead, one missing after whale-watching vessel,
Leviathan II, *sinks off Tofino,* BC

Rain-lidded dawn opens. Stage lighting
sieves thorough a scrim of cloud
from pitch to pewter to aluminum sheening.
Sea-blood scent, sting of brined iron

sieves through a scrim of cloud.
Who's the protagonist? Out there
sea-blood scent, sting of brined iron.
Glaucous gull flits like an eyelash along the coast.

Who's the antagonist? Out there
whale fins sew the great Pacific.
Glaucous gull flits like an eyelash along the coast.
The audience troops to port,

sea lions straight-stitch the great Pacific.
Oohs and aahs. What happens:
the audience troops to port,
on the tour boat, *Leviathan II,*

oohs and aahs. What happens?
Bent to view velvet mounds of sea lions
on the tour boat, *Leviathan II,*
shallow Plover Reefs. Passengers,

bent to applaud velvet mounds of sea lions,
weigh the port side down
onto shallow Plover Reefs. Passengers
on a twenty-metre vessel rolling,

the port side weighted down.
Open Pacific swells. Until a wave,
silent to the twenty-metre vessel rolling,
slams the starboard quarter, flips the script.

Open Pacific swells. Until a wave
stops laughter in the scrim light,
slams the starboard quarter, flips the script,
comes unseen from stage right.

Laughter stopped in the scrim light.
On the black rocks, lions bark, seas roar.
Coming unseen from stage right,
the Rogue's performed before

on the black rocks, lions bark, seas roar
sweeping down the boards. Oblivious.
The Rogue's performed before,
taking the bow, the curtain call.

Sweeping down the boards. Oblivious.
Cue light: pitch to pewter to aluminum sheening
taking the bow, the curtain call
on a rain-lidded dawn. How it opened like a stage,
    lighting.

PACHINA BAY, ʿANAQTLʾA

... places with which the heart exchanges glances
~ Tim Lilburn, *The Larger Conversation*

Problematically, I love stolen land
~ Corinna Cook, "Yukon Dispatches:
Writing from Art in the Changing North"

Three weeks we spent camping on the beach
        the woman who ran the campsite
        fed us homemade huckleberry jam on bannock
no visitors there in early July but us
watching our children play endless tag with pacific waves
the long beach walks   crystalline light   skin salted
buffed by sand   loose-limbed
the summer before us   spacious
a floating place of drifting whales
and, may I say, I felt
what I imagined a Huu-ay-aht felt
before first contact   I cannot claim
First Nation because I'm not   to this place
and no amount of imagining
can take me fully in or back,
though, I wonder if it might
take me a little way across
                        say

the coast unpeeled
each nacreous layer
allowed a porous space
sifted edges into silver light   sea   sky
pellucid union   sensed
by this deep-dug settler
in this only place.

Paddling that isolated lake.
The insulated park wardens, family of four.
The empty campsites perched on a cliff
far above the moody, unwelcoming wavelets.
Tiny in our red canoe on that glacial deep
and green. Fruitless hunt for fish, fleshless,
unwanted sticklebacks were all we caught.
You casting off the right gunwale, me the left,
the swish, the fly line lit in evening sun
sighing its silver length along the desolated lake.
Hungry pursuit of trout, a storm chasing us
down the long, scratched surface we're supposed
to see ourselves in. That arm *clothed in white samite,*
mystic, wonderful rising from the mere
to receive Arthur's sword. How much
have I lost to Romance? How much gained?
Samite, heavy silk woven silver. Silver flashing
around our campfire, and the lake's voice
full of rumble, uncertainty
and the tent intent on pulling up stakes.
Next morning the caretakers, makers
of a friendly end-of-season myth –
that we were wanted,
that the lake wasn't wanting –
why did I think of childlessness?
As we drove away, the pursuit
of longevity, desire for life, even more love,
and oblivion blowing us down the long road home.

REWILDING

Let the little girl, living amongst bears
and, schooled in avoidance, be undaunted

by a bluff-charge, though her mother be afraid.
Let the architects design apartment blocks

with nest openings for cliff swallows
and let beavers paddle downtown marshes.

Let the coyote stroll shopping districts unmolested,
the cougars pad city hills to cull the deer at night.

Let the foxes return to eat the white-footed mice,
bearers of ticks and Lyme disease.

Once I fished a river not far from the city,
a black bear fishing a distance downstream.

We locked eyes for an instant, stayed in place –
alertness brightening the blood,

making the Kingfisher's blue flash above the river
miraculous.

I hold the door for the mother with two girls,
No, thank you, she says, *they like to push the button.*
Magic. As electricity does the muscle work.
The millions of gallons stopped for this button,
the villages drowned, salmon re-routed, coal dug and burned,
nuclear waste shot into the heavens. *Wheee,*
say the little girls as the door swings slowly open,
and they race outside, gulping the particulate air.

Fourteen years at her helm,
forgetting land-locked alarms, becoming
taut arms, muscled back and supple knees
breeze-drenched, glazed in holy high seas,
leaving dirt, leaving trees, becoming clutched line,
bladed keel, tipped mast, becoming wind,
sinuous sail. The sailor, skilled tailor
of every inch of his boat,
sail-mender, tender of Kubota engine,
surgeon of buried wire, maestro of repair –
his edge luffed into loss.
Waves of giddy emptiness –
release from the burden to maintain –
yet tethered as age crashes
against those spiked shores.

ONCE WE WERE ANIMALCULES

i

We sail hard down Haro Strait flapping chart
   paper-weighted
by kellets the colour of February sky.

Husband hoots from the wheel as I bend at the bow,
yodel to Dall's porpoise surfing lacy waves.

They plunge, twirl, turn slippery torsos to eye
my face filmed in their salty exhalations

slick backs galloping
now here now in an instant   gone

     air mist-laden   rocking.

Where porpoise were a sudden kelp forest
long rust strands cling to the skull of a reef.

I shout to the skipper who hauls to port so sharply
   I almost tumble,
almost fall to drowned ribbons and the warning
   of porpoise.

Ah, to have forgotten about rocks the colour of ruin,
to have fallen so foolishly into a sea-smitten day.

     Once we were animalcules,
       tiny swimmers in droplets of sea.

Maybe it's the way we become,
laving in rubidium waves,

become sodium cesium copper
become fluorine cobalt gold.

ii

Our ancient selves return to us as
otters like the one I met in a grotto

secret hollow away from everyone.
Late afternoon tucked in the shallows

I read in my kayak while the otter
brought mussels to crunch

in a cave beside me, unnoticed for hours
my scheming mind lost in deliquescent time

            adrift.

iii

And that boundary-less day
young Harbour seal bobbing beside.

Two fathomless eyes
so close for so long looking.

Rhythmic waves of wet breath.
We wanted to say something:

pup becoming mercury pesticide
becoming toilet flush storm drain

a whisker away until heart-shaped nose
butted my soft-sided kayak   vanished.

iv

        Maybe it's the way we un-become:
4 a.m. anchored in an empty Sound
throat rinsed in warm black

silence battened in hemlock,
thick as stars sugaring the sky.

Moon rind wavering on the sea
as if lit syllables lick the hull.

One shriek   surprising as death
owl-caught mouse perhaps a mink.

The silence without people
palpable and heavy as the ocean floor.

v

What is home?
Try 70 per cent of earth's surface
cradle to three-quarters of all life

try names of things   sculpin orca tide
try sounds   heron's prehistoric caw

try original crawl from amniotic egg
with its own ocean sac   return

not ashes to ashes but
drop to drop   mist to mist

on a brine-drenched bow
I am soul from old Norse, *saiwaz,*

meaning belonging to the sea
meaning stopping place before birth   after death

     meaning
     tabula rasa is blue.

LAMENT OF A HYPOCRITE GARDENER

A friend has a raccoon water cannon
to protect her man-made stream
from night marauders,
pond-plant bandits scooping fish,
leaving a terrible mess.

The beasts hosed each night
like protesters by police.

— * —

I watch a TV documentary.
From a rock-strewn ravine
on an island in the Bay of Naples,
a gardener conducts rhapsodies
of Belladonna lilies, Birds of paradise.
A backlit day shot shows translucent veins
lacing sunblood through fleshy leaves.

I adore these exotics
transported from their wilderness
in the bowels of ships.

— * —

At a cabin by a lake
I've left the cedars to grow,
though they drape the water view
     tint green the light
sprinkling native salal.

My patch of less-touched
leaves deer to wander, cougars to prowl.

The neighbours love to look
across and see what once was.
All around the shore, their squat
lawn mowers gargle and spit.

— * —

In suburbia, though, I dig out pink Lavatera,
plant Lucifer crocosmia – fire engine red.
I fence the yard from deer, trap rats.

At garden parties, I point out to guests
the hummingbirds who dip their tongues
down the perfect throats of my cultivars.

PIPE DREAMS

By the beaver lodge bull rushes parade,
and pond weed floats in lacy clusters.
Mallards clap green bills through lily pads,
sieve clouds of tiny shrimp.

The park warden twirls a blade of spear grass,
grates its edge along his stubbled jaw, says,
he'd like to move the beavers to Beaver Heaven
for all the trouble they cause.

He's unblocking the beaver-stuffed PVC pipes
long ago shoved for water control
into the edge of the marsh
now used as a home by new beavers.

All around the lake, weeds rot,
grasses seed and bloom on fallen nurse logs,
roots drown and the silver skeletons of trees
descend into microscopic life

but these pipes, the promised plastic
of my parents' generation,
are pristine as the day they were made,
no trouble, no trouble at all.

THE LAST DAY OF THE PARIS CLIMATE
CHANGE CONFERENCE, I GO TO A BEACH SPA

Warmed pool perched above barnacles,
seaweed, seal-slaps, and the sucking tide.
Clouds like bleached towels
dropped on a blue tile sky.
We soak in heated salts
while December's metal sun
frosts the rising vapour.
A woman with kelp-brown hair glides by.
A florid man bobs. We dip
from steam to bubbly tub to mineral pool,
lounge on submerged ledges
like empty jackets on conference chair backs.
We melt to puddles while an engine
in the hotel basement pumps and pumps and
who deserves this? Who doesn't want it?

WHAT DOES WATER WANT?

~ for Duncan

Bowed as a prayer in a bay
sun sheening its back,
water slow-heaves,
breathes wishes.

We swim Pendrell Sound,
Melanie Cove –
where island-enclosed ocean rises
and falls, tidal as lungs.

We kayak, cupped red leaf
on Black Lake, once-logged.
Hemlock spurs rot below,
feed a patient hunger.

— * —

What does water want?
So little it shares another's colour –
evergreen emerald, algae rust,
the turquoise of silt.

— * —

We fished a river,
caught cutthroat for dinner.
Where a stream flushed over granite,
poured into spangled sunset.

We bathed naked,
soapless and laughing,
drank its cold,
and left.

— * —

Late fall and rain plays games of silver jacks
on a pewter sea. Pummels clean
a brine-drenched bow.

— * —

Winter water wants to soak down slow.
The sea asleep under rain's silky pelt.
People-less. Days, months of this
hiss, softness breaking cliffs.

A botanical term: when nature repairs,
layers over human traces –
seed in a puddle, scrap of dirt.
Will we be here to see it?

My body bucks before sleep.

Poems in *Water Quality* appeared in the following magazines and anthologies: *The New Quarterly*, *The Fiddlehead*, *WordWorks*, *Sweet Water*, and *Refugium*.

The W.S. Merwin epigraph is excerpted from "Rain Light" from *The Shadow of Sirius*. Copyright © 2008 by W.S. Merwin. Reprinted with the permission of the Permissions Company, LLC, on behalf of Copper Canyon Press, www.coppercanyonpress.org.

The Roger Kaye epigraph is excerpted from "What Future for the Wildness of Wilderness in the Anthropocene?," National Park Service, last updated 6 August 2016, https://www.nps.gov/articles/aps-v13-i1-c9.htm.

The Liu Waitong epigraph is excerpted from "Looking for Woodbrook Villa on Pokfulam Road" from *Wandering Hong Kong with Spirits*, translated by Enoch Yee-lok Tam, Desmond Sham, Audrey Heijns, Chan Lai-kuen, and Cao Shuying. Copyright © 2016 by Liu Waitong. Translation © 2016 by Enoch Yee-lok Tam, Desmond Sham, Audrey Heijns, Chan Lai-kuen, and Cao Shuying. Reprinted with the permission of the Permissions Company, LLC, on behalf of Zephyr Press, zephyrpress.org.

Many of the poems in "Fragrant Harbour" were included in a suite that was a finalist in *Exile Quarterly*'s 2021 Gwendolyn MacEwen Poetry competition.

"Diamond-Water Paradox": The Galileo epigraph comes from his letters to his daughter found in *Galileo's Daughter* by Dava Sobel (London: Fourth Estate, 1999), 152, and reproduced in the University of Chicago Press Journals.

"Master and Man" and "Eight Imitations of the Poet Wang Wei": Quotations in both poems, including "Farm Garden Happiness no. 4," are from *An Album of Wang Wei*, translated by Ch'eng Hsi and Henry W. Wells (Hong Kong: Ling chao xuan, 1974).

"Like a Moth to a Flame": The Mao Zedong epigraph comes from *Quotations of Chairman Mao*, compiled and translated by the People's Liberation Army.

"Hike on Lantau Island, 1968": The reference to Mary Hopkin is from the song "Those Were the Days" (*Post Card*, Abbey Road Studios/EMI, 1968).

The Gertrude Stein epigraph is excerpted from *Tender Buttons* (Toronto: Book*hug Press, 2008).

"Burnt Pot, Riverbank, Indifferent Sky" was a finalist for the CBC Poetry Prize in 2014.

"On Taming Foxes": The Antoine de Saint-Exupéry epigraph comes from *Le Petit Prince* (Paris: Éditions Gallimard, 1999).

"Slant Rhyme for Orchid": The William Shakespeare epigraph comes from *Measure for Measure*, 2.1.41.

"Argument with Captain Vancouver ...": The excerpts from Captain Vancouver's journal are quoted in *Passage to Juneau: A Sea and Its Meanings* by Jonathan Raban (New York, NY: Vintage, 2000).

"Rogue": The headnote comes from a CBC Online report dated 26 October 2015.

Pachina Bay, ʻAnaqtlʼaʼ": Epigraphs are excerpted from Tim Lilburn, *The Larger Conversation: Contemplation and Place* (Edmonton: University of Alberta Press, 2017); and Corinna Cook, "Yukon Dispatches: Writing from Art in the Changing North," *Assay: A Journal of Nonfiction Studies*, 1 November 2018, https://assayjournal.wordpress.com/2018/11/01/yukon-dispatches-writing-from-art-in-the-changing-north-part-1-of-4.

In "Nameless Lake," the quotation is from "Morte d'Arthur" by Alfred, Lord Tennyson, line 31.

The book *Water: The Fate of Our Most Precious Resource* by Marq de Villiers gave me much scientific knowledge about water, including the sobering fact that all the water we'll ever have is here.

I'd like to acknowledge death: the great waker-upper. It's slapped me up the side of the head a few times, but especially in 2005. Each time it reminded me to use the fear and get on with it (in the words of Auntie Claire, featured in the poem "Burnt Pot, Riverbank, Indifferent Sky"), with both the discipline of writing and the practice of kindness. So I want to thank death, or rather the dappled light of it, its stimulating intimation, not its arrival. Thanks go deeply to my initial family: Ralph, for his joie de vivre and sense of adventure, Phyllis, for her huge, loving heart and bookish self – wordsmiths, both – and Diana, my sister, for her companionship along several bumpy roads.

I searched for a writing group that, like Goldilocks' porridge, was just right – that magical combination of supportive and galvanizing – and I've found not one but two. Thanks go to the WWs (Barbara Pelman, Anne Hopkinson, David Pimm, Pam Porter, Wendy Donawa, and Barbara Black) and to the FBs (Patricia Young, Julie Paul, Arleen Paré, Yvonne Blomer, Christine Walde, and Barbara Lampard). Special thanks go to Anita Lahey who edited the initial phase of this collection, Yvonne Blomer and Patricia Young, who offered an expert polish on many of the poems, and Jan Zwicky, who dissected ten of the lake poems. Thank you, inspirations all.

Massive thanks to Carolyn Smart, Alyssa Favreau, cover designer David Drummond, and the fantastic creative team at McGill-Queen's University Press for their tremendous care and attention to this work.

Finally, and fundamentally, my gratitude, always, for Duncan, my greatest adventure and patient first reader, whose gifts for story, metaphor, and generosity are astonishing. Special thanks also to my daughter, Justine, and my son, Quinn, for their occasional perusals of poems, constant encouragement, and abiding love of language. And, in the order they also became beloved and supportive family, for Laura, Grayson ("Are you thinking what I'm thinking?"), Fred, and Hunter (welcome HQ!), whose favourite word is "ball."